In Her Words

Through Her Eyes

Poetry and Reflections

Gladys Elizabeth Patrick

Edited by M.D. Anderson

For Legacy

For family and friends

For those come and gone

For those here and those to be

And a bit of something just for me

Contents

Forward

As I reflect on my grandmother, Gladys Patrick, I think about the things I admire. She has lived a life rich in experience. A life comprised of part adversity, part perseverance, part joy. Found within the pages of her story I see the human mechanism at work. Too often we see others and ourselves as a title or series of titles: parent, grandparent, mother, father, child, sibling, sister, brother, uncle, aunt, son, daughter. Our inclination is to assign how we believe reality should be based on those titles. This sparked the question: Do we see who a person really is without the title? This is a question to ask ourselves as it relates to how we see, not only others, but ourselves as well. We are indeed the sum of our experiences in navigating life. This is the lens through which I attempt to see my grandmother.

I think of where she has come from and what she has accomplished. I think of what she enjoys now, at this stage in her life. She finds pride in reciting her poetry and writing poetry whenever inspiration comes. I admire the simple pleasures she enjoys such as watching old movies, soap operas, and her wrestling shows. She enjoys visits from family and being able to share her poetry. She especially loves going to worship services in her building where she shares poems and her favorite bible stories. What I see is the sunshine these activities bring into her world. And within her smile, I can see a well-earned peace.

This collection of poems comes from what is on my grandmother's mind. Her 98 years of living has given birth to these reflections as what could be described as "folk poetry". Much like African American folk art is derived from the experiences of a people influenced by history and culture and delivered in a raw nature, her poetry can be seen in similar fashion. She expresses how she feels and what's on her mind as it relates to her life experiences. Her offerings give us insight on life from her perspective. In reading her work you will

see her connection to family and faith and
the importance of practicing compassion
and understanding towards others.

M.D. Anderson (Grandson)

An Introduction

My name is Gladys Patrick. I was born on a farm near Rome, Georgia on June 24, 1927. I came to the city of Detroit when I was eleven years old. After graduating from Gillies Elementary School, I went back to Georgia. Shortly afterward, we moved to Dallas, Georgia where I attended Irma F. Matthews High School. I had finished the ninth grade and was halfway through the 10th grade, when my grandfather died. My family then moved to Detroit. Shortly thereafter, I went to work.

I met my husband at my friend's birthday party. Three months later, he asked me to marry him. I said no and he said, "yes you will." We did. We had five children. My first little girl was stillborn. I had five brothers and three sisters. After 20 years of marriage, my husband and I divorced. I constantly had the desire to finish school. I got my inspiration from Pearl Bailey, when I heard she was going back to school at the age of 50. I thought if she can do it, so can I.

I started going to GED classes for about a year. My counselor helped me fill out my grant papers and I am now going to college. My ambition is to become an artist. I like playing the piano and writing poetry. My hobby is growing vegetables in my backyard. I really love a beautiful garden of vegetables and flowers.

Gladys E. Patrick
Speech 101 Class
Wayne County Community College
January 21, 1986

About Me

There are several things I would like others to think of me. I enjoy helping people who are in need. I am determined to try and help solve the confusion in my church that has been going on for some time. I would like to put my creative talent to good use. I am pleased when my pastor asks me to help with the services in someone's absence.

I am happy when I can help someone solve their problem. I have a next-door neighbor that is handicapped. I run errands for her such as buying medicine and other things she needs. I have another neighbor with arthritis. I do light housework for her and another older lady that I keep company in my spare time.

I am determined to get an education for myself. I would like to be able to help my grandchildren whenever they ask me to help with their homework. I really don't like the idea of being ignorant.

I would like others to think of me as a person with creative talent. I am planning on finishing my art course. Art is the favorite of all my talents. I am amazed at the finished product. We are working with live models. I just hope to live up to my expectations. Although the college has dropped music, I intend to continue taking piano lessons. I plan on playing for my church when I am good enough. I love writing poetry. I hope in some way people can relate to it.

An Example: What Alcoholism Can Do for You

Alcohol is a disease
Alcohol can hurt you
But alcohol can do no more
Than what you let it do

A little shot did me no good
About this I do not lie
I would fill my glass up to the brim
To make sure I got high

And when my family came around
I hid my bottle on a shelf
And sometimes when I was not too cool
I hid it from myself

I find I cannot fool my friends, my children
Especially my mother

She would say cut that out
Straighten up and get yourself together

She said alcohol is no good
You know that it's a sin
You don't know where you are coming from
Much less where you have been

I hate for people to tell me
What I did and said the day before
Because if I could
I surely would just sink right through the
floor

It's time we got wise and try to help
ourselves
Because we have got a chance still
Because if we don't, God help us all
Because nobody else will

You can only hurt yourself
You make your loved ones cry
So you had better stop that stuff
Or else you are gonna die.

Gladys E. Patrick
Creative Writing Class
Wayne County Community College
Excerpts from Essay IV
April 11, 1985

Today
Can You Dig It?

I'd like to start the day off right
There's so much I've got to do
Well, If I worked both day and night
I doubt I would get through

I've tried so hard to get out of debt
I never seem to win
Just when I think things are straightened
out
They twist back up again

I've got my utilities all paid up
So I'm beginning to relax
Then I get a letter in the mail that says
"Hey what about your tax?"

My pocketbook is empty
And my bank account is closed
My money is so feeble
I just don't know where it goes

It seems I just can't make it
In these days and times
No matter how you figure boys
A dollar ain't worth a dime

I'm trying this and working on that
I'm on a budget yet
No matter what I do It seems
I can't get out of debt

I can't get extra work today
You know that that's a shame
My wallet is so wounded
I can hardly stand the pain

And now today is ending
This is all I've got to say
I'm glad there's no tomorrow
Cause I can hardly live today

That Was Then and This Is Now

Back then you could walk in and out of your
house
Day or night, without a key
Now some folks fix it where they need a key
To get in and out of your home
Which could create a problem you see

Back then you could crawl through a
window
Or a doggie flap
There was nothing wrong with a thing like
that

In those days you could buy 5 pounds of
sugar for one thin dime
Now 2 pounds of sugar cost a dollar ninety-
nine
Prices these days seem and awful crime
Cause a dollar these days ain't worth a dime

Old master say,
"Gal, I own you so you gonna work when I
tell you to"
Now the girl says,
"No baby you better pay me or I don't work
nothing for you"

Then, a child would attempt to do
something wrong
And his parents would chastise him and tell
him no
Now the child rebels with,
"You better leave me alone or this gun will
blow"

See, things were different way back when
Well, this is now and that was then

Life

Life is a period when good men suffer

Life is a period when happy men cry

Life is a period when the best men have it tougher

Life is a period when some men die

Rolfe, Portrait of my late husband by Gladys E. Patrick

What's Going On

When things you want
You cannot find
When you are late for church
You are left behind

When you press your light
It does not shine
When you are not a wild animal
You are humankind

When you bully your friends
You have crossed the line
When you can't find your way
You have lost your mind

I Mourn for My Lost Love

(Inspired by the movie: The Man in the Iron Mask)

My Soul's bound up in links of chains
My demented ego's consumed in flames of shame
I mourn for my lost love

I hurl my body against the jagged stones
But only my mind absorbs the wounds
I mourn for my lost love

I beat my head against the dungeon walls
My wails of pain echo down these hallowed halls
I mourn for my lost love

Depression

Something's always going wrong
Sometimes my mind seems almost gone
All my nerves are so uptight
My stomach aches
My dreams can fight

All night long I cannot sleep
I'm counting wolves instead of sheep
That goes on from day to day
Utilities, tax I got to pay

I try to do the best I can
It seems my friends won't understand
And when I tell my children what to do
Instead of listening to me
They listen to you

Sometimes I'm depressed
I don't know why
It's too late to cry
And too early to die

Always There

The Lord is with us all the way
To hear our prayers night and day
To help us through our ups and downs
To put a smile in place of a frown

You can talk to him at any time
He always listens, never a busy line
No call waiting, or putting on hold
To him your problems can always be told

When everything seems in utter despair
Talk to him, he is always there
Ask of him, and help will come
From the very rich, to the poorest one

No matter your face or color of skin
He shows no difference among all men
When trouble or torment in your heart lay
Just lift your eyes to Heaven and pray

Give God the Praise

Rejoice forever more
Use your power in God
To help someone

Do not close your ears to God
You must be patient
To all men

Some of us as old as we are
Live long enough
To prove our enemies wrong

I'm a Teenager

Old folks and parents are like an old floor
mat
They don't know what's happening
They don't know where it's at

They always want to know where I'm going
And where I'm coming from
They act like I don't have a mind of my own

They think I'm not listening
My feelings don't show
They are always telling me something
I already know

They are afraid I might listen
To the wrong kind of teens
That might talk me into doing
Some unlawful things

Like drinking alcohol and taking drugs
A kind of addiction I would never begin
That would lead me to stealing
From my parents and friends

Please don't you take drugs
Just don't begin
Because it will surely lead
To a deadly end

My parents say please protect yourself
And don't be in a hurry
Like having two or three children
Before you marry

I know that they love me
I remember what they say
But I still got some things
I am going to do my way

Bully

There seems to be someone
That's always waiting around
To make you feel uncomfortable
Always putting you down

The name of that is bullying
I think that is right
They make you feel useless
And try to keep you uptight

They always pick on
One person at a time
I think that's unlawful
I would call that a crime

How could they be happy
By making someone cry
And making them feel helpless
By telling them a lie

God wants us to forgive them
Some folks wonder why
Jesus wants us to love them
Let us promise we will try

Prisoner

We can't forget the things we do

As we live our whole life through

Please remember this my friend

That I'm a prisoner just like you

If

If I could find the good man
If I could find a helping hand
If I could find a wonderland
Then I would be wealthy

If I could give you peace of mind
If I could give you love divine
If I could only make you mine
Then I would be wealthy

If I could grant your slightest wish
If I could fill your life with bliss
If I could give you all of this
Then I would be wealthy

We Are Somebody

Listen up I'd like to make this clear
If we wasn't somebody we wouldn't be here
As men and women let's not fail to see
That we are all created equally

When black people marched
On a non-violent scale
They were beaten and whipped
And thrown in jail

They had struggled with equality
And had wrestled with pain
They were led by this great civil rights
leader
Whose name was King

In one of his speeches, he shouted
Out with a blast
"Free at last, free at last
Thank God almighty we are free at last"

Our God wants us to forgive our neighbors
Faithfully in the belief that he will forgive
you and me
Let's pray and ask our young men all over
this land
Just pull up your pants and be man

The Harvest

We must sow some seeds of
encouragement
Plant some seeds of hope
Sing songs of joy and happiness
And help someone to cope

We share our blessings with others
Less fortunate than we
It flows like a river
And spreads like the sea

We give to the charities, to the homeless
Those of poverty and despair
We give our time, some clothes, some food
To let them know we care

We show our neighbors friendliness
With a wave or a smile
Our caring can lift the spirits
Of some lonely hearted child

On the highway of life
At the end of the road
Where the seed of the young
Reaps the harvest of the old

Stand Up

Stand up and be counted
For those who may not see
Proclaim that Jesus is alive
And he's alive in me

Even when the going gets tough
And the way seems hard
Stand up and be counted
Among the real children of God

Now when you hear the words stand up
Don't just stand on your feet
Put on all of God's armor
For you have evil to defeat

In the strength of God, you can make it
Yes you can
Romans chapter 14, fourth verse declares
God is able, to make you stand

So, when the devil comes along
And tries to make you give up
Announce that you're a child of God
And He will help you stand up

Example For Men

There's a place in this world today
It's a challenge for fathers
And millions of good men

I would like to find that place
And the medicine
That could make men better

Men who would be
A good example
For their wives, sons, and daughters

An inspiration that demands
Respect and everlasting love
Jesus did his part
So, it's time we do ours

Out of Touch

When I see you every morning rushing off
to catch the bus
All the things I'd planned to tell you: Loving,
caring things and such
Hey, your smile's a thing of beauty, but
you're always out of touch

So many times, I waited for you to come
home or even call
Many days and nights I waited, and you
didn't come home at all
I am longing to be with you and just loving
you so much
Hey, your smile's a thing of beauty, but
you're always out of touch

Sometimes I think I hear your footsteps
come running down the hall
I get up to rush and meet you and there's no
one there at all
Don't you know how much I love you and
I'm needing you so much

Hey, your smile's a thing of beauty, but
you're always out of touch

Now you've gone away and left me and I'm
missing you so much
Child you know I'll always love you and I'm
hurting oh so much
May the Lord God bless and keep you
Now that you're really out of touch

(About my late son Philip)

My Son Philip portrait by Gladys E. Patrick

Spring

Like a beautiful maiden fair
Once again there's a newness in the air

Spring is here with glorious days
Flowers and trees in stunning ways

Babbling brooks and birds that sing
Spring is such a wondrous thing

In this beautiful peaceful glade
I see wonders my God has made

The world's aglow with glorious rebirth
I pause and admire this living Earth

My Guiding Light

In this world that I now live
I'm really glad, glad that I can give

Some wisdom that was taught
To other folks that God has wrought

Mom was surely a wonderful teacher
Her love for the Lord was a daily feature

In showing us how we should always live
To make others happy and constantly give

Thanks to my mother and our Lord above
We are spreading his word and giving our
love

To all we greet out on the street
And to those around us that we meet

My Mother

Just like sunshine every morning
Just like midday every noon
Just like sunset every evening
Just like love that's full in bloom

Just like love can conquer heartaches
Big or little, large or small
So my mother loves her children
With all our faults, she loves us all

Just like flowers bloom in season
Just like Autumn leaves that fly
Just like knowledge from the old man
Just like wisdom from the wise
Just like love can live forever
Something pretty never dies

My Mother, Lucille White

Happy Birthday Brother

I have a brother
Who's friendly and kind
Sometimes I think
He could read my mind

His family thinks
He's number one I've heard
He loves me and helps me
Without saying a word

Father's Day

What is a father?
He is a hard-working man
Who is willing to give his wife and children
A helping hand

He's a man full of good advice
When he asks his children to do something
He doesn't like to ask twice

He says, when you work for someone
Do the very best you can
And they will always
Want you back again

Fathers say, don't smoke
Don't drink, don't steal
And don't get in a car
With a stranger behind the wheel

Another of his sayings
Which might be true
"Do as I say, not as I do"

We celebrate Father's Day
In our own way
I say, every day
Should be Father's Day

Christmas

Christmas is the time of year
Where everyone likes to spread good cheer
We shop for clothes, we shop for toys
And stuff for good little girls and boys

If someone's Christmas things are stolen
Please let your neighbor know
They will help you collect some clothes and
toys
More than you had before

There's one good thing about America
When people have suffered a loss
Let it be known to your friends and
neighbors
And they will come across

Happy New Year

Let's say Happy New Year to everyone
We are blowing our whistle
And beating our drum

We are skipping
And dancing
And singing our song

Singing joy to the world
The Lord has come

We are needing our Savior
More and more everyday

While we are fighting sickness and prejudice
Which seems here to stay

Let us pray for our family
Let us pray for our friends
Let us pray for this world
That this evil war ends

Our Friend

Today, we are having an Appreciation Day
For our Resident Service Coordinator
A well deserving lady

You all know the story, we know is true
That we must give credit where credit is due

She works between two senior apartment
complexes
Very helpful and caring, she's as good as it
gets

When she spots an ambulance, she's on her
way out
To see who is sick, to find out what it's all
about

She will make it her business to see where
they go
Get in touch with the family, make sure that
they know

If someone is sick, she will go to their rescue
She is a woman who listens, then figures
out what to do

She is so good at helping the seniors out
Whether some of them want her to help
them or not

After explaining their problems, she gives
100%
Of her time and energy to take care of it

She is rushing here and rushing there
It seems she is almost everywhere

Well, I've said it all, there's nothing left
I hope she's not so rushed that she runs into
herself

Our Pastor

He's been through the fire
He's been through the rain
He's suffered betrayal
He's suffered some pain

He's conquered heartache
He's balanced the scale
He's overcome hardships
Where others have failed

He's carried his burdens
Sometimes alone
And embraced the courage
To carry on

His strength is waning
His steps are slow
But whenever he's needed
He's ready to go

God bless his efforts
God bless his name
With all his sacrifices
He remains the same

In His Own Time

God moves in His own time
He has wonderful patience
And gives us so many chances

To learn of him
And trust
And love
And forgive each other

When we finally
Open our minds
To his goodness
Then mercy comes in

We can only receive forgiveness
When we forgive others
For we have all sinned
And come short of His Glory

Thank You Lord

Thank you Lord
For sending your son
Into this world of sin

To give your children
A second chance
To start all over again

Then as we gather on this blessed day
While pausing to say grace

With all that's going on today
And what we have to face

About Me Part 3

I hope to reach the goals of my life with my studies and my willingness to work at it. I would like to accomplish something worthwhile in my lifetime, so that someone might think well of me.

Gladys E. Patrick
Creative Writing Class
Wayne County Community College
Excerpts from Essay IV
April 11, 1985

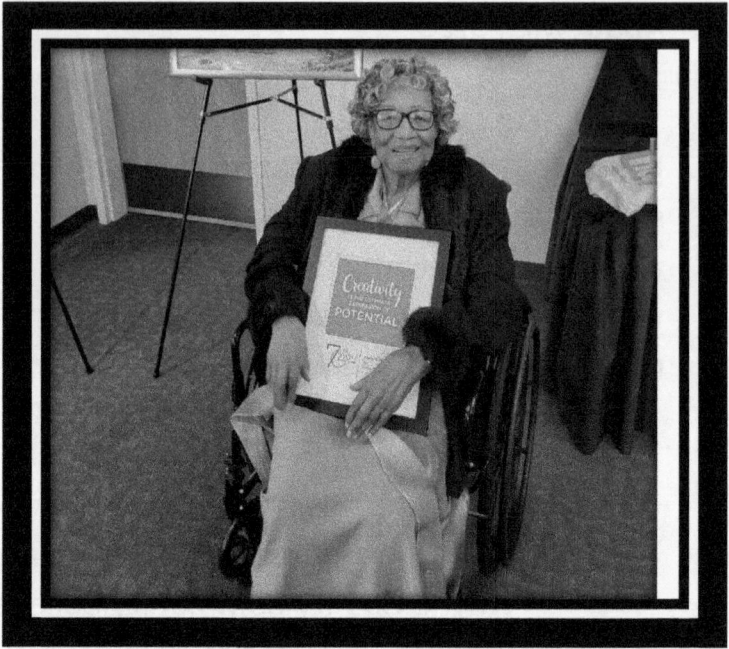

Hannan Center's 70 Over Seventy Awardee Class of 2023

Top: Flyer for her first ever art exhibit featuring her favorite personal work of art, My take on Blue Boy.
Bottom: Reading poetry at the art exhibit.

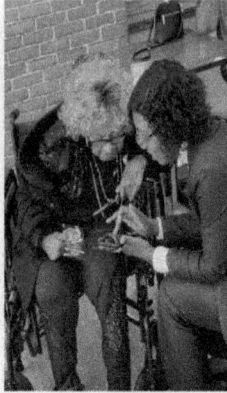

Her Flowers

Now

Biography

Ms. Patrick is a recipient of the 2023, 70 Over Seventy Award through the Hannan Center in Detroit, Michigan. She is an artist, poet, and storyteller. As a child of the Great Migration, she was born near Rome, Georgia on June 24, 1927, and moved to Michigan in her teenage years. The primary lesson of her journey is the perseverance it took to maintain doing what she loves. She has faced much adversity in her life. With no moral support or encouragement and during a time where her work was considered raising 4 children and keeping the household together, she found time in the late-night hours to draw, paint, and write at her kitchen table.

In her late 60's she attended classes at Wayne County Community College and Marygrove College. This is where she found an outlet with like-minded individuals and instructors who gave her the room to explore and create. She thrived in her art and creative writing classes.

Glady Patrick's resolve is evident in her work and in what she has accomplished. She overcame childhood abuse, alcoholism, and the loss of two of four of her children before their time. Her lifeline has been, not only her creativity, but her ability to share that creativity with others. In addition to sharing art and poetry, she loves sharing stories from her life and her favorite Bible stories.

She continues to make an impact by sharing her poetry with church friends, fellow senior community members, and family at various events. She is the go-to-person in her community for people needing an uplifting poem shared or written.

Her impact is not limited by age but enhanced because of it. Her journey is a lesson in not only finding joy but sharing it. Her work is timeless and an inspiration for all ages.